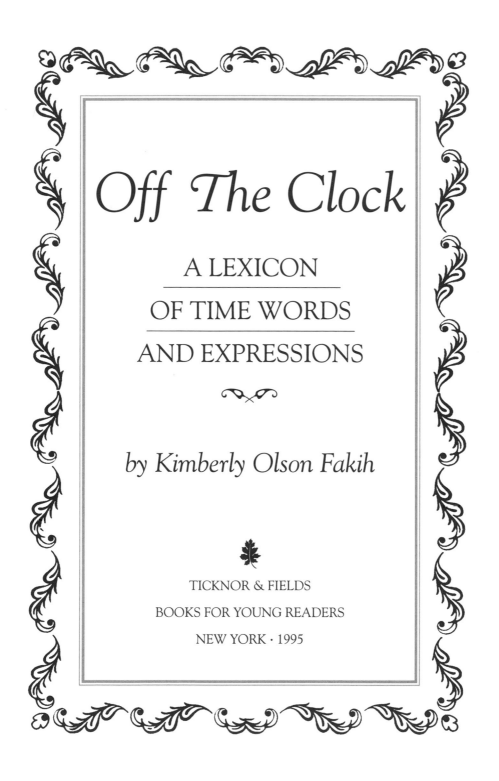

Off The Clock

A LEXICON

OF TIME WORDS

AND EXPRESSIONS

by Kimberly Olson Fakih

TICKNOR & FIELDS

BOOKS FOR YOUNG READERS

NEW YORK · 1995

Published by Ticknor & Fields Books for Young Readers,
A Houghton Mifflin company, 215 Park Avenue South,
New York, New York 10003

Manufactured in the United States of America
Book design by David Saylor
The text of this book is set in 12 point Goudy Oldstyle

VB 10 9 8 7 6 5 4 3 2 1

Library of Congress Cataloging in Publication Data
Fakih, Kimberly Olson.
Off the clock : a lexicon of time words and expressions /
by Kimberly Olson Fakih   p.   cm.
Includes bibliographical references.
ISBN 0-395-66374-1
1. Time, Words for—Juvenile literature. 2. English language—
Terms and phrases—Juvenile literature. [1. Time, Words for.
2. Time. 3. English language—Terms and phrases.]
I. Title.   P326.F35   1994
428.1—dc20   94-2082   CIP   AC

Off The Clock

Old English May Day Revels

Time—
An Endless Song

Some people know what time of year it is by the candy in the stores: if candy corn is in supply, can Halloween be far behind? Peppermint canes mean the December holidays are near; hearts, of course, are for Valentine's Day; and jelly beans herald Easter.

Others watch the sky for the first "V" of geese heading south to signal the oncoming fall and winter, no matter how warm the days of an Indian summer might be. Scientists believe that the annual navigation of the birds is linked to the seasonal position of the sun in the sky.

Sometimes time has more to do with feelings than with measurements. No matter what the calendar says, for many people it just is not winter until the first snow, nor is it spring until the appearance of the first robin redbreast of the year, or, in some parts of the world, the first sighting of storks circling overhead.

A clock is a peculiar tool—and a confounding one. We say it "keeps time" for us, but actually, it is no more useful than any other measuring tool, such as a ruler or a scale. But clocks do come in handy. When a group of friends want to meet, they need to specify an hour on the clock so that everyone shows up at the same time. Like street names that tell them what corner to stand on, a clock gives locations to the hours in the day.

Clocks measure time. Clock time is generally "quantity time." But if clocks are always about time, time is not always about clocks—among many things, it is about "quality time." And it is about the feelings people have about their days—to feel hungry and know it is time to eat (though the hour for lunch has not struck), or to feel sleepy and know it is time for a nap (regardless of what the clock says).

People of all age groups and eras have had in common the ability to experience and "go with" the rhythms of the day and to understand the orderly passage of each day and night, even if no cuckoo clock screeches forth the hours. Think how absurd a clock face would be to a baby: the dial would have very few "hours"—milk time, nap time, burp time, poop time.

For people the world over, nearly all the hours of the day have associations that everyone knows and understands. Dawn is the time for rising, for bird song, and for celebrating the sun; nightfall, which comes at a different moment every evening and used to mean the hour the gates of towns and villages closed, is the hour for shutting down, going home, turning on lights, and thinking about bedtime and the next day.

The *words* for time, not *numbers*—lively expressions instead of hard-and-fast dials or digits—can add to what we already know about time, to our experience of it and shared familiarity with it. A selection of these words and phrases makes up the entries in this lexicon.

Time is so much a part of everyday language that it is hard to utter a single sentence without its somehow coming into the conversation. In English, verbs have tenses, meaning we place our actions in time: they happen in the past, present, or future. If we try to leave time out of the conversation, we cannot speak for long. Some people have gone so far as to say that time is like water all around us that we swim in but are mostly unaware of.

While time has been around "since the beginning of time," a mechanical clock is relatively new. Until six hundred years ago, when the timepiece that most closely resembles what we now call a clock made its first appearance, people looked to nature—the sun, the stars, the seasons, the ebb and flow of the sea, and the flight of geese—to tell them if it was time to plant, time to reap, time to marry, time to prepare for frost.

These days, it is harder to live only by nature's time. Even farmers, who are more tied to the land and nature's rhythms than the rest of us, must know the dates and hours their local granaries are open, the time schedules of the trains, trucks, or planes that ship their wares, and other details of the business world. The modern world demands that we follow clock time in order to program our VCRs, time-stamp our faxes, arrive at school and work in a timely fashion, and know when stores where we shop close.

Under such conditions, time that is "off the clock" looks downright luxurious. It is not. It is present every time two people become friends or fall in love (not because the clock or calendar tells them to), every time we wake up before the alarm goes off because the sun is streaming in the window or the snow is covering hill and tree, and every time yet another apple blossom unfurls in spring.

Aion

Once upon a time—no one knows just when that was, but everyone seems to agree that it was very long ago—there was a child god, Aion. This Greek name-word is one of the earliest mentions of time, presented as a living, breathing child, playing fancifully amid sandcastles at a beach, rather than as a rigid object like an hourglass or a precise mechanical object like a clock.

"Aeon" or "eon," derived from "Aion," has come to mean a period of time that is not measured exactly by clocks or calendars—an eon can last from several years to hundreds of thousands of years.

Almost everyone is accustomed to the less formal use of the word that indicates a chunk of time: when people are anticipating a happy event or simply waiting in line to go to the bathroom, even a few moments can seem like eons.

Bee time

Like most workers, bees have specific times to do their tasks. But there is no hurrying them up or slowing them down; they set their own pace. Bees are naturally punctual: they visit flower beds at the moments in the day when the nectar

is good and ready, and just when plants fling their pollen into the air.

Some bee watchers believe that bees keep time by "reading" the position of the sun in the sky, but no one knows for certain. When French bees, accustomed to foraging at a certain hour, were brought to New York, they did their work on Paris time.

Blink

People do it all the time, and almost everyone has attempted not to. The blink—the rapid closing and reopening of the eyelid that takes place thousands of times each day—was once the smallest unit of time. People still use it to describe something that happens fast: to blink is to miss it ("it happened in the blink of an eye").

Scientists use much tinier segments to measure time, but the duration of the blink has been nailed down: it takes about 1/5 of a second.

A "jiffy" is another word that means a very short duration of time. It is not much longer than a blink, but the origin of the word is unknown. Even though everyone knows what "I'll be ready in a jiffy" means, how long *is* a jiffy? Perhaps it is yet to be decided. Unlike a blink, an actual movement of something (the eyelid), a jiffy cannot be measured.

Calendar

The word "calendar" means a system or method people use to divide up time. A calendar is also something to carry around, bearing photos or pictures and purchased in a store. Many people glance at it for information, but hardly notice the photograph or picture that accompanies each month. In the past, people took such decorations far more seriously; during the period of time known as the Renaissance, an elaborate "Book of Hours" (called the *Très Riches Heures du Jean, duc de Berry*) was created for the brother of the king of France. The illustrations chronicled the countryside activities of peasants and nobility through the year.

A century earlier, a calendar made some people so angry that they marched in the streets. In 1582, Pope Gregory XIII realized that the calendar used at that time (known as the Julian calendar, developed during the reign of Julius Caesar) was inaccurate. He wanted to use a more precise system. But it meant cutting ten days out of the calendar for that year, and some people believed they were actually losing ten days of their lives. With shouts of "Give us back our ten days," they protested. But the Julian Calendar Change, as it was known, is now a part of history. And the world has lived with the new Gregorian calendar to this day.

July in the Très Riches Heures du Jean, duc de Berry

The Gregorian calendar is a solar calendar, calculated according to the revolutions the earth makes around the sun. Another way of measuring the year is the lunar calendar, based on the cycles of the moon. Jewish and Islamic calendars are lunar.

Other calendar systems have come and gone. The ancient Druids, early inhabitants of Britain, used measurements of both the sun and the moon, a "luni-solar" calendar. Every eight years a full moon appears on the longest or shortest day of the year. Time-keeping methods developed at places such as Stonehenge may have been charted from this event.

There is no one calendar that all or most people of the earth agree on. Followers of each calendar can claim that everyone else is off the mark, and, in some ways, they would all be right. No one calendar is more right or true than any other.

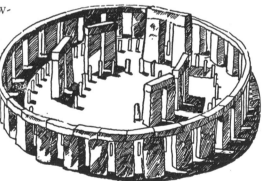

But if a calendar can make people feel angry, it can also make them feel glad. In rainy April, a glimpse of the sunnier months of June's and July's pages can be cheering. Students and teachers can look forward to the end (or the beginning) of the school year, or back upon the accomplishments of the season just past. Those who write appointments on their calendars can look at old entries: a short scrawl may remind them of many pleasant hours. A calendar is more than just a way to measure a year: it is a chart of the ways we spend our days.

Canonical hours

Long before clocks were in use, people relied on daylight and darkness to tell them when to get up and when to go to bed.

About fifteen hundred years ago, a system of keeping time known as canonical hours began in monasteries and other religious centers and continued until the Middle Ages. Throughout each day and night, bells

called out the hours of official prayer for those inside the walls. The bells could also be heard by people in the towns and villages that often sprang up around such holy places. Their days were thus segmented, too, but not

only for prayer. The hour of Prime, at sunrise, became the hour at which the gates to the town might be opened, and the hour of Vespers, at sunset, signaled that the gates were about to be closed. The ringing of Vespers also meant curfew, the time when decent folk returned home to pull the shutters across the windows and bars across the door. Nighttime streets were left to the criminals.

Habits associated with each canonical hour have become more general. Vespers, which once meant the time for prayer held at sunset, now means evening service in the Eastern Orthodox Church and their beginning of the day. The same service is called Evensong in the Anglican Church. "Vesper" is also a name for the evening star, and a vesperal breeze is a gentle evening wind.

The meanings of the words have also changed. "None" once meant midafternoon prayers but has become the hour of high "noon," and the hour of Prime usually means the segment of the evening when the largest number of people watch television.

Not only a pattern from a distant time, the present day's divisions are mainly the result of the regular call to worship several times each day that may have begun with the canonical hours and their equivalent in various religions. The familiar way we think of our days as morning, noon, afternoon, evening, and night, or, more simply, breakfast, lunch, and dinner, is not based on the clock, but perhaps on very old tolls.

THE CANONICAL HOURS:

Matins (midnight, signaling the
    lengthiest period of prayer in the day)

Lauds (prayers at first daylight, no direct
    sunlight yet)

Prime (sunrise)

Terce (midmorning prayers in the hours
    of full daylight)

Sext (noon, sun directly overhead)

None (midafternoon)

Vespers (sunset)

Compline (for prayers said before
    retiring)

Cock's crow

A very old phrase that is one of the most enduring ways to refer to early morning. Everyone the world over knows that the rousing racket at cock's crow means it is time to "up and at 'em."

Five hundred years ago, in Europe, soldiers took their roosters with them to the battlefields, so they would get up in time to fight.

The ancient Greeks also used the cock as dawn's messenger to mark their days. They substituted the word "dawn" for "day": "He will get there in two dawns."

Christ told his disciples, the night of the Last Supper, that before the cock crowed, Peter would deny him three times. Peter obliged. But he more than made up for it, by establishing what is called Mother Church.

Perhaps the most famous rooster of all is Chanticleer, who appears in one of the stories in *The Canterbury Tales* by Chaucer. This bird was known for his accuracy with his daily bugle.

Cock Crow

Cycle

In nature, a cycle is something that keeps happening again and again at regular intervals: the sun rising every morning, the tide washing over the beach rocks as it goes in and out each day, the dogwood trees blooming every spring. There are cycles of many kinds, some big and some small. They are fairly reliable ways of time-keeping.

Every time Earth rotates on its axis, throwing most people into a period of light and a period of darkness, one day-long cycle is complete. One lunation, or moon cycle, means a full month of the lunar calendar has passed. And the passing of winter, spring, summer, and autumn marks the cycle we call a year.

Sowing, growing, and harvesting is a crop's cycle. The biological cycle of some animals, such as sheep, causes them to bring their young into the world each spring.

In a cycle of every seventeen years, cicadas (locusts) hatch, climb trees, make the forests a-whirr with their noises, mate, and then die.

There is also a one-day cycle—the lifetime of the mayfly. It is born, matures, and dies in the space of a twenty-four-hour day.

Wheel of time

Plants with annual cycles are called perennials; they regenerate (grow again) year after year. Some species of bamboo bloom only once every seven years.

The cells of the human body have cycles, too. Many of our cells divide in cycles that are as regular as the ticking of a clock: every two years in the liver, and as frequently as twice a day in the lining of the gut. Mature brain cells don't divide at all, having but one lifetime cycle.

The cycle is often thought of as a wheel—the wheel of time. It is sometimes shown as a snake (or a dragon) eating its tail, which indicates the nonstop motion of a wheel.

Dawn

Dawn has always been a time of great hush, and great violence. Gray sky turns to pink in this in-between time that marks the end of night and the onset of day. Birds twitter their early morning chorus, while in quiet corners, morning prayers are uttered.

Duels to settle small disputes usually took place at dawn. When the disputes were large, battles over the centuries began at first light and continued until the stars were visible, for the simple reason that before

gaslight, electricity, and modern enemy-spotting equipment, the fields of war were too dark at night for fighting.

Dawn has also been the traditional time to carry out the executions of convicted criminals, whether by the gallows, electric chair, firing squad, or whatever grisly means popular at the time.

Dawn is not only a time of doom and dying, but of growth. All living things grow ten times faster in the morning than at any other time of day. The human body is biologically programmed to get a second wind in the morning, even if a person has been up all night, cramming for a test or jamming at a slumber party.

Another word for dawn is "daybreak." At daybreak on St. Lucia's Day in Sweden, the oldest (or youngest) daughter in the family rises before everyone else, dons a wreath of lighted candles around her head, and takes coffee and saffron buns to her parents and other adults in the household. The December feast day reminds all Swedes that the long, dark days of winter will soon wane, and the sun will once again climb in the sky.

Day

"Day" is a word we use so often that we almost forget what it means. For most people, a day starts when they open their eyes in the morning and is over when their  heads hits the pillow at night. But the word can include both night-time and daytime, and while almost everyone agrees that the day is about as long as it takes for the earth to rotate once, not everyone divides the day into twenty-four segments, called hours. In the Hindu religion, a sacred Brahma day is one that lasts about four thousand million years.

The Aranda people of western Australia say that each day has twenty-five parts. In ancient times, the Sumerians had days that were divided into twelve segments; the Babylonians twenty-four; and the Egyptians twenty-six, naming each after one of their gods. After approximately 660 B.C., the Japanese segmented their days into fifty *koku*s, with each koku consisting of six *bu*s.

For people in China long ago, one particular calendar had more than seven days in each week and therefore more than seven names.

The day itself, in one old Chinese system, could be divided into one hundred *ko*, each one lasting for what is now fourteen minutes and twenty-four seconds. In another system, the day lasted from midnight to midnight and consisted of twelve segments. Each of these segments was given the name of an animal; for example, because of where it landed in the 11 p.m. to 1 a.m. slot, what is called midnight was said to be contained in the hour of the rat.

These days, even those who live their lives "on the clock" may count days differently. Bank days are a little shorter than many other work days and have given us the phrase "banker's hours." Travelers may have to adjust twice: if they change time zones they may suffer jet lag (their bodies will say "bedtime" while their watches say "midday, do not stop yet"); adding further

insult, the hotel day is quite short, generally from 2 p.m. check-in one day to 10:00 a.m. check-out time the next.

As a unit of measurement, a day is easier to keep track of than minutes or seconds, in the same way that dollar bills seem easier to keep track of than pennies. Regardless of how it is measured, a day can feel long or short. Some days are so busy they seem over before they start, and others (like the fifth rainy day in a row) can feel endless. When people want to spend time outside, a sunny day looks like a promise ready to unfold, while a cloudy day seems like a threat hanging over their heads.

Day keepers

A day keeper, according to the Qiché Indians of Guatemala, is someone who tells others how to use their days well, the same way a good coach might show players how to play well by enjoying the game and putting their hearts and souls into it, or the way a good teacher might get students to read more or to love a certain subject, rather than just memorize facts and do homework.

Keeping a record of the day, diary-style, can involve jotting down upcoming appointments or quietly recording noteworthy events. But the Qiché, descendants of the Maya, are more demanding of their days: their day keepers help others live a "full life" by guiding them to spend each day as if living were an art—the equivalent of painting, composing music, or making a poem. Any activity, no matter how dull, can be done from the heart, with joy, and every task performed as if for a loved one, in step with the earth and the pace of the seasons.

Perhaps that is too poetic for most people and too hard to do. But many do believe that a little time well spent is more important than much time wasted. It is now a fashionable idea, also known as "quality time," but it sounds as though the day keepers knew it all along.

Daylight saving time

Though more about time on the clock than off, daylight saving time is an annual shift ahead one hour on an early Sunday morning in spring, which often results in people showing up late for church or other appointments. Adults accept it as normal; most kids encountering daylight saving time for the first time want to know where that hour goes. In the fall, the clock is shifted again, this time back one hour.

Once again, a time expression can highlight the fact that clock time seems like a game or a convention, just a laid-down set of numbers that everyone agrees on—and for most of the United States, they even agree to shift it around twice a year.

Dillydallying

The wibble-wobbles of time can be unclear and vague, and even a little risky. Someone who pays too much attention to time may get nothing else done, but anyone who pays no attention to it whatsoever and "stops to smell the flowers" can be accused of all manner of misconduct just for hanging out.

But dillydallying, though considered mere idleness by adults, can be a legitimate and even necessary way for kids and teenagers to fritter away their hours. A luxury usually reserved for youth, it looks like loitering, and for poets, a chance to "while away" time. Clearly, dawdling is in the eye of the beholder.

Dog days and dog nights

The dog days of summer are those droopy, dripping, sweaty days in the later part of the season when, for some, the thought of shopping for itchy wool school clothes makes Chinese water torture look refreshing.

The origin of the phrase has nothing to do with the sight of neighborhood dogs panting on front porches. As the story goes, the morning star, also known as Sirius the Dog Star, rises with the sun each day and joins its heat with the sun's, making the days sultry. The ancient world agreed on this and believed that dogs were likely to go mad during this time.

In more recent days, the phrase "three-dog night" is, for certain regions, a customary way of describing a time of frigid weather by stating how many dogs one should sleep with to keep warm. A one-dog night is on the balmier side; a three-dog night is a real bone-chiller.

Donkey's years

It is not that donkeys (or raccoons in the expression "coon's age") have such long life spans—by animal standards, they are quite ordinary. But somehow both animals became associated with phrases that mean "a long while," and once in a while, someone uses these phrases.

It is probably no coincidence the phrases "donkey's years" and "donkey's ears" sound so similar; if you say either phrase several times you are more likely than not to end up pronouncing the other. And they both refer to rather lengthy flaps.

The able-bodied donkey also appears in stories of midwinter celebrations in old Europe. It often bears weary party-goers and revelers who have overdone it to a resting spot known as oblivion, where they would stay for quite a while. To "sit upon the donkey with your face to the tail" may reveal something about keeping our eyes on the past as we go forward in time.

Dreamtime

The Australian aborigines believe that dreamtime is a place, the original place where the world begins. Not only do they believe that they leave homes and beds, the trees they sleep under, or the bushes they happen to doze in, but also that they return from their travels as different people.

Anthropologists call this mythical time. But the aboriginal belief in dreamtime is no less holy than others' beliefs in heavens or fairies, or that the world was created in six days. The world was created—and is being created still—in dreamtime, the aborigines say. They call it the *Aljira,* and think that the time they spend dreaming is more real (and therefore more important) than their waking, daylight hours. Dreaming is the source of all art and all things sacred.

Ecological time

Ecological time may sound like the hours people spend recycling and performing other jobs related to protecting the environment. It really means dealing with nature's time—its seasons, yearly cycles, and transformations—rather than man-made time, the clock. The clock on the wall rushes on without regard for things like weather, light, or species.

The expression "ecological time" was first coined by the English anthropologist E. E. Evans-Pritchard.

Nature's time means that there is a particular time in which an apple ripens or a rose blooms. No clock can be set to a rose's course: from bare bough to leaf, to bud, and then full bloom. No one can say that it takes roses four months, nine days, seven hours, and sixty-six seconds to swell into bloom; every rose unfolds in its own time.

People cannot control ecological time or slow it down to suit their needs, though some try to beat the clock by growing off-season tomatoes in a hothouse or cabbages in such places as Biosphere II in the Arizona desert.

Often, people can do no more than observe nature and live with its rhythms. Anxious to plan their planting seasons, farmers with good sense—and a good sense of humor—pay tribute to nature's grip by hanging around a groundhog's homebase in February to find out how much winter is left.

Elevenses

Most entries in this book explain words and phrases that existed *before* there were clocks, or without reference to clocks, but not this one. Eleven o'clock was once a set time for tea (*see* "Teatime"). People referred to the activity first as "eleven o'clock tea," and then as their "elevenses," as in "Have you had your elevenses yet?" Now, although tea may be served, elevenses can be any light snack around midmorning.

Epoch

When people want to describe a long period of time that has come to be associated with a particular idea, a particular event, or series of events, they might choose the word "epoch." NASA, Apollo, Sputnik, moon orbits, and Mars expedition plans have given the name "the Space Age" to the period that began in the 1950's. "The Space Epoch," though not as catchy, could also be used.

In a sense, epoch means an "age of" or a period of time, such as the Renaissance, the Middle Ages, or the Jazz Age. It is derived from a Greek word (*epochē*); a related word in German is *zeitgeist*, which literally means the spirit of the times.

To understand zeitgeist and epoch better, perhaps it is helpful to consider one of their near opposites—"anachronism"—that roughly means something that is *not* in the spirit of the times. In Washington, D.C., a medieval cathedral is being constructed by masons, artisans, and other old-world craftspeople using old building methods. Modern equipment and conveniences have been discreetly tucked away, as if to tease onlookers about where this cathedral belongs in time. It is an anachronism, out of place in time.

Equinox

Its effect is hardly noticeable, and most are unaware of it, but two times a year the sun crosses the Equator (the

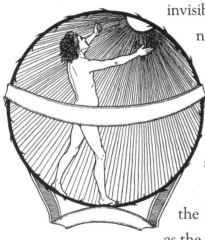

invisible ring around Earth's middle, neatly dividing it into two hemispheres, or half-spheres), making day and night the same length. On the modern calendar, this happens once around March 21 and again around September 21.

Following the spring equinox in the Northern Hemisphere (also known as the top half of Earth), daylight begins to outstrip nighttime, and the sun is said to be growing to manhood, or so thought the ancient Druids of England and Wales.

As the days following the autumn equinox grow shorter, with the hours of daylight decreasing, people sometimes say the night is "closing in" on them.

Eternity

No dictionary can explain what the word "eternity" really means. No one has been there, and no one even knows if such a thing exists. We assume it does, but we cannot prove it.

Eternity sounds like something so far away that even a super-spaceship might not be able to come near it or find it. But some, like the ancient Greeks, used a peculiar expression to talk about it: they called it the "eternal now." They claimed that eternity is actually right here and right now, the only time there was, is, and will be, without beginning or end.

All this means is that some folk have believed there is no yesterday or tomorrow, only today. If a girl wants to ride a pony or eat six ice cream sundaes in a row, she can do it only now; she cannot do it in the past because the past is already out of reach; and she cannot do it in the future, no matter how determined she is, because the future is so far ahead she cannot grab it or touch it.

If two people were to argue about whether time stays the same permanently or changes all the time, do not place bets on a winner. They would both be right. Time has two basic features: change and permanence. Some people say that change is eternal and permanence is eternal and have compared time to a river: the waters are ever-changing, rushing past, but the river itself is always there, always the same. In fact, thousands of years have passed since people first argued about time matters, but no one is any closer to understanding what time is, only that human beings are always right in the middle of it.

Evening

There is no more favorable word for describing this window of time between afternoon's broad daylight and nighttime, which is more closely associated with bedtime. Evening can be the time for play, snacks, television, or homework.

Unlike some other words that describe a time of day (sunset, dawn), evening is not necessarily linked to the sun's position in the sky. Summer evenings seem long and light, especially for those who observe daylight saving time.

Eventide

An old-fashioned term for evening that is not often used, but at one time meant the time of day at which the chance for company was possible but not guaranteed. The American naturalist H. D. Thoreau quoted the words of a sacred Hindu text on the visitor who never comes: "The house-holder is to remain at eventide

in his courtyard as long as it takes to milk a cow, or longer if he pleases, to await the arrival of a guest." Thoreau actually waited long enough to have milked one hundred cows, but no one ever came.

Events

Before there were mechanical clocks, before people could say, "it happened at half-past," some people used (and still use) events as a way of noting the passage of time. The Hopi and Sioux have expressions that tell them only whether something happened before or after a specific event—an important event, not one of the hundreds of small, trivial events that happen every day. They have no words for time or that indicate time, and verbs in the Hopi language do not have past, present, or future tense. To note a child's day of birth, they might say it happened "before the big famine" or "after the crops were flooded."

According to this way of marking time, time is not roped into written-in-stone periods. Instead, it is tied to things that happen that break up the ordinary rhythms of daily life. Any day can be broken up into errands, chores, interruptions, and delays. Each day has a pattern of events: playtime, before school, recess, mealtime, naptime, after school, television time, before-dad-comes-home time, after-mom-goes-to-work time, and so on. A girl could not say that something happened "the day I ate a bologna sandwich" unless she hardly ever ate bologna sandwiches—only then could it be considered eventful.

When an event is rare and important enough to have lasting effects on the lives of the people involved, it is highlighted and becomes a time marker, such as the time before the divorce and the time after the wedding.

In India and China, people still regularly talk about the path of their own lives paralleled to great events that took place in their neighborhoods, towns, or villages.

Even historians have been known to abandon arithmetical tabulations and declare that this or that happened after the fall of Troy, or after the Ming Dynasty collapsed, or since the Flood, or during the time of the dinosaurs. No one will mistake the time or era of certain events, so leave the dates at home for these: Creation, the Last Supper, the Crucifixion, the American Civil War, the Depression, the fall of the Berlin wall.

An event does not have to be once-in-a-lifetime to

be of importance. The planets in our solar system occasionally seem to line up in space, forming a beeline to the sun. This incredible astronomical event is called "syzygy." It is a passing phenomenon, but unlike a solar eclipse, people often associate it with fortune, magic, and serendipity—happy accidents.

To the children of a tribe in Guinea, there exist only times of good fortune, good and happy events, or unfortunate times that beget unfortunate events. Instead of today, yesterday, tomorrow, last year, or three years from now, they have only two times: favorable ones and unfavorable ones.

First time

There is a first time for everything: the first visit to a dentist, the first time one loses a tooth, or rides a bike with no hands.

The first time an athlete jumps higher or runs faster than anyone else is jotted down in the record books. The first time a child makes an appearance in the world is cause for yearly cake-and-candle festivities; when that child is Jesus Christ or Buddha or Martin Luther King or Alexander the Great, the annual celebrations become a little more significant. A first time leads to an annual noting of that event, and it may become part of a cycle.

In everyone's life there is a list of first times around which anniversaries, birthdays, and other occasions of special note are constructed and celebrated.

To the Iatmul people of New Guinea, many first times are regaled, such as the first time a boy sharpens a spear, his first hunt or catch of a fish, or his first sighting of an opossum in the bush. But a first time does not have to be firmly fixed in our minds—we can remember such pleasant hours as the first time we made a friend, read a certain book, tasted apple pie, or saw a shooting star without recalling exactly when it happened.

Peculiar to first times is that more often than not they cannot be predicted. When two people meet, they do not know whether they are going to become friends or not, or whether they will be celebrating that first date in the years to come. The first time someone receives flowers is not something that can be noted on the calendar before it happens. A "first" in sports can be prepared for, worked up to, and wished for, but it is no more than a dream or goal until it has actually happened.

A near opposite to first times are last times. When a bad thing happens for the last time, there is reason for rejoicing, but when a good thing happens for the last time, the occasion is often tinged with sorrow. Last times can slip by, sometimes without our notice until they are long past.

Flower clocks

To keep track of time, some have gone no further than the nearest flower. Different parts of a plant wilt at different times; each leaf and petal may have a separate rhythmic timetable, or life span. That is why some petals will fall off a flower even while its bud is still unfurling.

The Navajo placed flowers on a road to mark time; they knew by the withered condition of the blooms how much time had passed.

In 1727 a Swedish botanist named Carolus Linnaeus noticed that various types of blooms opened or closed at specific times throughout the day. He suggested the use of a flower clock, with flowers planted in a circle so they would reflect the passing of time:

LINNAEUS'S FLOWER CLOCK
6 a.m. Spotted Cat's Ear opens

7 a.m. African Marigold opens

8 a.m. Mouse Ear Waekweed opens

9 a.m. Prickly Sowthistle closes

10 a.m. Common Nipple Wort closes

11 a.m. Star of Bethlehem opens

12 p.m. Passion Flower opens

1 p.m. Childing Pink closes

2 p.m. Scarlet Pimpernel (Poor-Man's-
Hourglass) closes

3 p.m. Hawkbit closes

4 p.m. Small Bindweed closes

5 p.m. White Water Lily closes

6 p.m. Evening Primrose opens

A version of Linnaeus's clock

Garden

There is no better "off the clock" location than a garden. From its beckoning paths even the crudest mechanical clocks are barred, and no bumpkin or clodhopper would dare bring a digital timepiece. As the Mad Hatter says in Lewis Carroll's *Alice's Adventures in Wonderland*, "It's always six o'clock now," perhaps meaning that it is *never* six o'clock—it is never any time at all.

In books and movies, if not in real life, the garden is

A Renaissance garden

usually the place where people feel free, for a few moments, from their duties. It is a shelter and a resting place associated with leisure and relaxation.

In religions that have a belief in one god (called monotheistic), the garden is considered a place of innocence and timelessness. Adam and Eve's stay in the Garden of Eden was but a short one; it is always noon in heaven, and there is no timeflow (there is an innocence of the knowledge of time). Believers think that the descent from heaven was the real beginning of the time count.

The garden has been considered, literally, a piece of heaven on Earth. We have heard it said that a good garden cannot be rushed; no soil can be tilled until the time is ripe and the tiny vines and tendrils can do their work.

Gardeners plant trees for the sound the leaves will make in the wind or when spattered with raindrops, or for the dappled shade they cast. They arrange species of flowers to grow together that will please the eye by the way the colors contrast or complement one another, or by the grouping of tall plants and short ones. They choose fragrant plants and bushes whose blossoms will fill the air with scent. In China the garden walls are high and the grounds they enclose vast—sometimes they encompass entire vistas and landscapes. People have joked that the Great Wall of China is merely part of one gardener's grand vision. Large and small, some gardens require more work than others, but when the tilling and planting and hoeing is done, they are meant to be places of tranquility for meditation, strolls, and play, away from the sights and sounds where the clock reigns supreme. Where there is no garden, there is no place to rest.

If clock time is banned, nature's march of time is alive and well, bringing each garden to fruit. The garden is a living artwork that grows with the changing spectacle of nature; living "paintings" and "sculpture" continuously unfurl day in and day out, year in and year out.

Both people and nature take residence in a garden. Seasons pass, along with autumn deaths and spring resurrections, and crows and nightingales arrive and depart, but the garden itself remains, seemingly outside the domain of familiar time.

Hogmanay

Almost everyone hails the new year, each in her or his own way; for many people the last day of the year means a chance to cut loose before settling back into the daily grind.

In the Scottish Highlands they celebrate Hogmanay, a time of clamor, license, and feasting that is considered part neither of the old year nor of the new one. In olden times a man dressed up in the hide of a cow went from house to house, making loud noises and banging drums to keep the residents safe for the year ahead and to banish any remaining ill will from the year behind. He was chased through the homes by children with staffs, who were probably only too delighted to beat on his hide and contribute to the uproar. The celebrations were charged with great shouts and special bonfires.

This was also the time to receive the good omens of the new year, the time for renewal or regeneration or starting over. People adorned houses, perhaps with mistletoe or other harbingers of spring, and gave gifts, perhaps of winter aconite, a delicately colored blossom known to pop its head up from snowy banks.

Holiday

The first holiday to make most people sit up and take notice is their birthdays. The annual recurrence puts them in touch with the other cycles of nature and points out that they are growing older.

Although it is true that Santa time comes but once a year, it does come every year, making it part of a cycle of festivities that never changes. That certain events—not just birthdays, but Halloween, Valentine's Day, and more—keep popping up every so often shows how holidays and festivals are a way of marking time.

The holiday season in November and December (concluding January 1st) has less to do with dates than with a festive mood.

The Carnivale in Rio de Janeiro, Brazil, may start and end on specific dates, but in between, as the participants throw themselves into one of the biggest parties in the world, night and day begin to meld in the ongoing feasting, noise-making, and masquerading.

Thanksgiving, which was originally a harvest celebration linked to nature, was declared a national holiday in 1863 by President Lincoln. Once held on the last Thursday of November, a congressional act in 1941 placed it on the fourth Thursday of that month. President Franklin D. Roosevelt later wanted to change the day Americans celebrate so that it would not be so close to Christmas. He almost caused riots.

In the beginning

It would be nice if everyone could pin down exactly what they mean by "the beginning," but they cannot. That is because there is no real beginning—there is only what people *believe* to be the beginning, just a point in time that they all agree will be the beginning, in the same way that people "on the clock" agree to synchronize their watches to make them all show the same time. Some things become true only because everyone agrees they should be true.

The beginning, then, is the start of everything else, but it is not intended as a precise moment according to clocks and calendars.

Presenting Archbishop James Ussher.

In 1650, in England, this man declared that there was one and only one beginning and that he knew exactly when that was: it took place in 4004 B.C., on the 22nd of October, at 6 p.m.

The image labels read:

The first dayes worke. The seconde dayes worke. The thirde dayes worke.

The fourth dayes worke. The fifth dayes worke. The sixte dayes worke.

The Six Days of Creation

But the beginning, for everyone, depends on when they start counting. And when they start counting depends on what they consider a key event or defining moment. For example, the Christian calendar (the one most people happen to follow) begins with the life of Christ. The year A.D. 1 (or *Anno Domini*, Latin for "the year of our Lord") is the Roman calendar year of 753 A.U.C., or *Ab Urbe Condita*, a Latin expression meaning "from the building of the city," or the founding of Rome.

People stopped using the Roman year count, started

using the Christian one, and became so accustomed to it that it is now easy to forget that not everyone counts years the same way. Using the Christian calendar (including its usage here) as a point of reference is universally accepted, not because it is correct or true to do so, but because it is conventional—it is agreed upon.

The Jewish calendar began in the year equivalent to 3761 B.C., 3761 years "Before Christ" was born. The Islamic calendar's year 1 A.H. is calculated from the time the Prophet, who founded the religion, made a long march between the cities of Mecca and Medina (A.H. stands for *Anno Hegira*, "the year of the journey") in the year equivalent to A.D. 622.

An emperor was enthroned in the year equivalent to around 660 B.C. in Japan, an event that launched *that* calendar. In India a calendar dates from the year equivalent to A.D. 78 and is named for the king who founded a Scythian tribe at that time.

If there is a beginning, there must be an end—which is even harder to confirm. For many religions, an event called the coming of the Messiah may complete the calendar; the calendars of past civilizations—like the Romans—have met more ordinary fates. They ended by falling into disuse when

other methods of counting, like the Christian calendar, came into use.

In science, a calendar may go on indefinitely, without end. But that is another story.

Without a beginning or an end, what is left is the middle. One way to think of time is as being in the middle of a story in which neither the beginning nor the end is clear.

In sync

Secret agents make certain that their watches are synchronized; "in sync" means that no matter what measurement they use, they are on the same schedule, rhythm, or beat.

Most people know when they "feel" in sync with the world, so to speak. They are at peace, happy, content, hopeful; their breakfast was hot and delicious, maybe, and they had their homework ready for the day ahead. It is an all-around feeling of well-being. But in the natural world, synchronicity is not just a feeling—it is a biological fact.

Mother Nature needs no mechanical clock to make separate events occur at the same time. Many varieties of bamboo plants die at the same time in vastly different and distant parts of the world. The eggs of a South

American bird, the ostrich
tinamou, all hatch at once,
even though they were laid
at various times: the chicks
call to each other from in-
side their respective shells, until each of them is ready to
pop out its head at the same moment. In Southeast
Asia, there is a species of fireflies that all flash in unison.

But one need not go to a foreign country or into the
bamboo groves to find things that run in sync. The
heart's natural pacemaker has cells that, due to electrical impulses equivalent to tiny beats, run in sync and
tick uniformly to create one big beat. And each grain in
a packet of yeast (the ingredient that makes bread rise)
has a sugar "clock" inside it, so that whether the yeast is
dry and dormant or activated by water or sugar, it will
tick along in perfect harmony with its neighbors.

Judgment Day
or "The end of the world as we know it"
"Will time ever stop? Could time ever stop?"

People are always looking for signs, or omens, that
the world is ending. This is not a very happy outlook.

Every century has had nearly earth-shattering
threats, such as the plague in the Middle Ages or the

consternation over nuclear war in more recent times. Though the world has survived so far, people will always find a reason to believe that the end is near. And who knows? Someday, perhaps some of them will be proven right, if and when the world does end—whenever that may be. And if that is at all possible.

Such a period is also referred to as Judgment Day, the Apocalypse, or the Last Day. Those phrases mean that time has run out, is standing still, or has just plain stopped.

Kairos

Kairos is often pictured as a young man with wings. This musical-sounding word is a Greek expression that points to something that is often called "sacred time." It is not necessarily religious. It can stand for the instant or moment that is part of a turning point, such as the Big Bang (the moment that scientists say may have led to the creation of our universe), or the twinkling on Christmas Eve when Santa Claus descends down the chimney, or the moment of triumph when the winner of an Olympic gold medal is announced.

On a smaller scale, a student who realizes in one stunning moment that she is the top of her class, or a boy who has just experienced his first kiss—those are moments of *kairos*.

Whether measured in large chunks of time (that boy's kiss may last in his mind much more than the few seconds it took) or in those as small as a flash, a momentous occasion demands the full attention of human beings. It is unforgettable. In eastern India they call it the "fortunate instant," and the word for *kairos* is *kshana*.

Kairos can also mean the right time for decisive action, such as the daring moment when one adult says to another, "Will you marry me?"

Other expressions come close to the meaning of *kairos* as a taking hold of the moment of truth. The poet Horace in the first century B.C. coined the phrase "carpe diem," which

Tempus fugit: *time flies*

most people recognize as "seize the day"; this is not too far off from the expression "take time by the forelock," which roughly means now or never.

Kids' time

Days can be divided up according to clocks, but some people have a different system. The time to get up may be the moment of awakening, no matter what hour of the day it is. Mealtimes take place when hungry, and  "after school" can start at any time, as long as school is shut down for the day. Recess time seems to exist between bells or buzzers, and game time lasts until it is over, whenever that is. A tea party can be at any time and of any length. Quality time might be only as long as it takes for parents to talk to kids about their days, or it may last for a whole weekend. Curfew time can be as vague as "home before dark." A party or picnic can be scheduled to end at a certain time, but might last as long as there are guests having fun.

Kids' time may be in a head-on collision with parents' sense of timing. How long does it take to "stay in your room until you've thought about your behavior"? Or to get "good and ready to apologize for what you've done"? Or to "stay at the dinner table until you've eaten

your broccoli"? (For one stubborn child, the answer to all three questions was all night long.)

Still, there is help for the beleaguered. When parents say, "Come here this second," a possible response (although there would still be the question of propriety) might be "I'm on Roman time." Romans did not have seconds. They simply did not divide time into such small and petty measures. Egyptians did not even have minutes. A command loses most of its urgency for those who talk like an Egyptian: "Come here in this hour of Horus!" Who's going to hurry?

Lifetime

A word usually associated with various lengths of time, a lifetime can last one day or more than a century. Only when it is over can the span of a lifetime be measured by clocks or calendars.

Several lifetimes ago, a Japanese monk named

Dōgen said, "Life is more transient than dew." Since "time flies," even the longest lifetime is temporary—absolutely impermanent. He believed both animate (men, monkeys) and inanimate (pebbles, mountains) things have lifetimes.

That might be true of the mayfly, whose entire lifetime extends no longer than a day, but it is also true of those turtles that can live for over a hundred years, and of trees, like cedars, oaks, or redwoods, that may live for centuries.

Light

It may seem obvious, but the only thing separating the time we call night from the time we call day is light. Almost every living thing is influenced by light.

Plants grow toward the light, turning their leaves in the direction of a sunny window; chickens lay more eggs during the long days of summer, and the eggs will hatch faster if placed under artificial light.

Before the invention of the clock in the late Middle Ages, the hours of work were mostly regulated by sunlight. If people toiled from dawn till dusk, they worked

Sunflower, a living sundial

longer days in summer than in winter. But perhaps it was not an obvious fact to them and the days did not necessarily feel longer; or, if it was, and they were counting workdays rather than work hours, perhaps they did not give it much thought. They were simply in tune with nature's rhythms and, summer or winter, a day's work was a day's work.

Give a dog a watch and he will probably slobber on it. Plants and animals may not be able to tell time, but they are better at tuning into nature than people are. Scientists say that plants or animals adjust to the intensity of light, which shifts not only during the day but during the year. That is why the slobbering dog will grow a heavier coat for winter when the weather is still warm and why a cat will begin to shed before the first buds of spring have unfurled.

Linear time and cyclic time

When only one thing happens at a time, never to be repeated in quite the same way, we say that time is linear, that it runs in a straight line, like a story that begins at the beginning, continues to the end, then stops. The timeline that is said to have begun with Christ continues, to the present and beyond, to an unforeseeable future or end.

Time's arrow

If linear time—which some people have called "time's arrow" because its journey is from point A to point B—is a one-way street, then cyclic time is almost like a carousel perpetually in motion, with the same seasons, holidays, and natural rhythms popping up again and again. That is why cyclic time has also been called "time's wheel."

For the most part, linear time can be oriented toward the future, with surprises around every corner, suspense among the cobblestones, and hope—and optimism—in every step of its unpredictable way. Cyclic time, by contrast, can be mostly focused upon the past, and thus may be predictable, often reassuringly repetitive, and perhaps blissfully reliable.

Ma

This word may mean "mother" in several languages, but in Japanese it is something of a temporary break in conversation or action, a meaningful one that can speak volumes. When we try to think of the equivalent of *ma* in English, the phrase "a pregnant pause" comes first to mind.

The ma in conversation is the time of silence between two words or two sentences, which, if done right (according to the cue of some invisible maestro), is full of significance no matter how long or short the pause.

It can also mean the blank time when a person is not doing anything, a time of not-doing: not eating, not sleeping, not playing, not watching television, not going to school, not anything that takes up time—an "off the clock" time. Thus, ma can be the break time or the empty time between doing this or that.

For the Japanese gardener, a ma is the empty space between two cherry trees or two rocks. But it is not just an empty gap; it is part of the arrangement and is considered as important as the objects themselves.

Perhaps we can only grasp this word if we take a moment's peace or stillness to "get it."

Marking time

So intent have people been on measuring time that there are dozens of clocks that are nothing like the mechanical one we are now accustomed to following.

In Korea, rope soaked in a flammable substance was burned as a fire clock; so much rope burned for so much time.

In both China and Japan, weights were tied to long wicks or fuses; as the strings burned, the weights fell off, signaling the passage of time.

Chinese joss sticks have been (and are still) broken up into parts and burned in a certain order; each part burned meant a certain time span hadpassed.

Japanese geisha houses burned *senko,* or what people call "flower girl incense sticks," as timers.

More than five hundred years ago, in fourteenth-century China, carved incense burners looked more like mazes than clocks. Incense with various aromas was placed in mazelike grooves and lighted; as it burned, different scents were released into the air, telling anyone with a nose for time of the hour.

A more basic time-marking device is the sundial. The crudest was little more than a stick poking straight out of the ground; people told time by looking at the stick's shadow, which changed as the sun moved through the sky. Scratch dials—marks tracing the sun's path scratched on the southern sides of churches (and often into the windowsills of houses)—were eventually created on separate slabs that were then attached to walls.

Another version of the sundial was a "noon cannon." Through an arrangement of glass and gun powder, this volatile timepiece was activated by the sun to go off at high noon.

Noon cannon

Finally, about alarm clocks (other than the celebrated rooster): messengers in ancient China took the idea of personal alarms seriously. They inserted sticks between their toes before sleeping, then lighted the sticks. These burned away, all the way down to the foot and then—! A scorched toe meant "time to go!"

"Time to go" is a phrase that can have more than one meaning. There is a tale of how one group of resourceful Native Americans made sure they woke up early in the day: they drank a large quantity of water the night before, turning their own bladders into internal alarm clocks. The pressure to urinate would rouse them, perhaps to head into battle or march to new hunting grounds.

Matinee

What time is a matinee? A theatrical matinee—an afternoon performance of a Broadway show—might begin at 2:00 p.m. But that is not the only kind of matinee.

In some regions of the United States, "matinee" is a word full of promise, originating from the midnight canonical hour Matins. It can be any outing during the daytime, or an afternoon event—movie, show, short meal, or a brief excursion into an ice cream parlor. It can be an afternoon gathering of a few good friends, a light snack, and some good talk.

Midnight

It is no wonder that the deepest part of the night has long been associated with malicious spirits that walk on the darkside. It is the time of bogies, hobgoblins, and pixies—the "witching hour" when the menacing dark rules the land. It is always midnight in hell, according to rabbinical tradition.

But midnight is not always pitch-black; in fact, there is little darkness at midnight in Scandinavia during the summer months. The sun never fully sets but seems to hover near the horizon.

It is the chiming of midnight that sent Cinderella running away from the ball, where she had danced as if in a timeless dream, and back into her real world of ragged clothes and wicked stepsisters.

Midsummer and midwinter

Midwinter and midsummer are general terms that can mean the two days in the year about which most cultures have invented stories of magic and myth. Midsummer is the longest day of the season; midwinter, the shortest day of the season. Both are associated with strange behavior and spooky visitations.

The English playwright William Shakespeare made much of midsummer in his play, *A Midsummer Night's Dream*. In that story, everything familiar is turned upside down: a man named Bottom begins the play fully human, but halfway through is transformed (his head, anyway) into a donkey. A fairy queen, usually scornful of human beings, falls in love with him. Only when the next day dawns is all set to rights.

For those living in the northernmost sections of the globe, midsummer is the centerpiece of what can be twenty consecutive days of daylight; the sun never sets.

On midsummer's eve the oak tree blooms, but, mysteriously, its blossoms wither before daylight. Peasants in some parts of Italy searched the oaks on midsummer's morning for what they called the oil of St. John, a resin that some people believe may be extracted from the sacred mistletoe which grows on, and gets sustenance from, the oak.

If midsummer was a time for public bonfires and celebrations, then midwinter was a time for a more private fire, the indoor burning of the Yule log. In parts of France, the log was burned on each of twelve days, and then kept under the bed for the rest of the year, protecting the household from fire and thunder.

The Yule log and the twelve nights later associated with Christmas (as in Shakespeare's *Twelfth Night*) came long before Christianity, which may have simply joined the story of the Nativity to the midwinter festivities already established by those who came before.

The Hopi of the southwestern United States hold a

nine-day midwinter ceremony called a *Soyal*. In modern times it is a celebration of the sun's pending journey back up through the sky, but in earlier days, prayer sticks were offered in thanks for the sun's return after its plunge toward the horizon. The prayers were carefully timed to when the sun started back toward its zenith, satisfying both astronomical laws and religious ones.

These goodly folk are not alone, however, in their regard for the sun; more than forty groups of native peoples in California alone were known to have been watchers of the big eye in the sky.

(*For more on midsummer and midwinter, see* "Solstice.")

Month

The word "month" is derived from the Latin word "menses," for moon. Far more interesting than the word's origins is that for thousands of years, people have watched the waxing and waning of the moon as one way of keeping track of such life-and-death events as the planting and harvesting of crops and the coming of cold and snowy seasons.

Others have watched the moon's phases in order to determine the right time for marriages to take place or circumcisions to be performed.

April

The lives of the ancient Egyptians were closely tied to the moon's rhythms. They thought of each month as having three sections: the waxing moon, the middle (or full) moon, and the waning moon.

The names we use for the months are Roman: March, from the word *Martius*, which is related to the god Mars; April from the word *Aprilis*, a month sacred to the goddess Venus and perhaps named for her Greek counterpart Aphrodite; May from the goddess Maia; June for the goddess Juno, or perhaps for Junius Brutus; July for the emperor Julius Caesar; and August for the emperor Augustus. September comes from *septa* for the seventh month (counting from March, when the Roman year began), October from *octo*, or the eighth, November from *novem*, meaning ninth, and December, the tenth month, from the word *decem*. Romans had only ten months. January and February were added later; the first is from Janus, the god of doors and beginnings, and the second from the Latin *februa*, or purification.

Just imagine if Americans, after the Revolutionary War two hundred years ago, had decided not to use the Roman names for months, but had invented their own. Perhaps they would have called April "Leaves Coming Forth Moon"; June, "Rose Moon"; July, "Blossom Moon"; or October, "Leaves Fall Moon." Such fanciful name-calling is just what happened in France after the French Revolution. In 1792, a new government temporarily adopted French names for months that translate to "Frost," "Snow," "Seedtime," "Blossom," "Harvest," and so on.

Other variations on what to call the months exist or have existed in places as far away as Siberia or as close as the Midwest, for instance, "the month of thawing snows" and "the molting of reindeer month."

Mørketiden

This Norwegian word means "the murky time."

In the northernmost town of Norway, residents are accustomed to alternating seasons of near-constant sunlight and near-constant darkness. The *mørketiden*, from November to the end of January, is grueling, even for those who have grown up with it.

During this sunless period of the year, the sky is continually dusky and gray. Children's grades drop, and so does the number of new pregnancies.

In the Scandinavian countries, the dark winter months demand game playing, festivities, and celebrations to keep people's spirits up. Perhaps when they are not partying, these folk dream of summer's midnight sun.

Nemawashi

Two or three people might take moments to decide which movie to see, or they might take much more than that. The Japanese word "nemawashi" means the amount of time it takes for a group of people to agree on something or come to a decision.

Nemawashi is finished only when it is finished and not a moment before. Perhaps the closest to an American nemawashi would be "It ain't over till it's over," or "It ain't over till the fat lady sings." In both expressions, a particular time stretch has an end not decided by the clock or some specified time, but according to what actually happens "on the floor" or "in the field." The importance of group participation, however, is more obvious in the Japanese expression.

Other cultures have similar notions. For one of the United States' native people, the Pueblo, the date set for beginning a dance is "when everything is ready," and only then, regardless of the weather, time of day, or what day.

But exactly *when* is everything ready?

It can take two hours, three days, or a week, but everything is ready not when the clock says it is, but when all the people involved agree that it is. This may not seem precise or accurate enough, but it is a very specific moment.

That makes the dance as unpredictable as a sneeze, at once providing satisfaction and release. It is a very special moment, an apparently spontaneous one, and looks almost as miraculous as everyone sneezing at the same time, only far more likely.

The Pueblo also build their homes at a time that translates to "when the right thoughts are present."

These ideas may sound uncommon, but the more familiar phrase "biding your time" is not any more specific. How long does *that* last? People believe that they will know, somehow, when the time for "biding" is past and the time for "doing" has arrived. When a grandmother says she will clean her attic when she "gets around to it" or when "the spirit moves her," no one doubts that it will be done. And it is done.

Night

Anyone who has ever been in a room where all light has been shut out can imagine just how long and dark nights were in ages past. These days, relief comes with the flick of an electrical switch and a nod to Thomas Edison.

Once, night was thought of as a mysterious time, the hours when suspicion and mistrust roamed freely and when terrible things could happen to unlucky travelers in the dark.

People's centuries-old feelings about nighttime have outlasted the dawn of electricity for a good reason. Darkness still provides a cover for mischief-makers and worse; more crimes are committed at night than during the day (and more still on rainy nights than clear ones). There are few unlighted places left in the world, but artificial light is less perfect or pure than sunlight, and it carves eerie shadows from the gloom.

The atmosphere at night is undoubtedly powerful— ask anyone who has tried to tell a ghost story in the full sun. In bright light, with the everyday noises of traffic, children playing, and people going about their work at home, office, school, and shops, a scary story just is not as frightening.

The more words there are in a language for something, some say, the more important that something is to speakers of that language. Arabic has thousands of words to describe a horse. The fact that there are so many names for the hours in the day—first light and sunrise, forenoon, midafternoon, dusk, and so on—and so few for night shows what "day" creatures people are. Night is really the only one familiar word, other than midnight, for all the hours of darkness between the sun's last glimmer and its first rays in the early morning.

An Antarctic night, or polar night, is not one night, but many. It lasts for five months of continuous darkness, from April to September, during which night and day are nearly indistinguishable. This is true in the Arctic, too, at a different time of year. At both poles, on the day when the sun finally returns to the sky, it sets moments later.

Under different skies and in various corners of the globe, nightfall is the hour when the cows come home, their udders full and ready to be milked. It is considered the end of the day and is also called "evenfall." In

Captives of Time, a book rife with details about the various changes clocks have brought into people's lives, dire events take place at nightfall, which begins with the tolling of Vespers. As one citizen of daylight declares, ". . . cutthroats have the town all night. It's ours again with the ringing of prime at sunrise." The author, M. Bosse, writes, "It was past vespers then, and only a dull glow shimmered on the river," showing how people of the fourteenth century, before the invention of the modern clock, might have thought of the day's passing into night.

Nine days' wonder

The artist Andy Warhol once said that everyone will be famous for fifteen minutes. Most people in the entertainment industry know this too well and work hard to stay famous for longer than that. But Warhol's words have all but replaced an older expression that means the same thing. Any person or event that was fleetingly part of the news or briefly in the spotlight was referred to as a nine days' wonder (even if the fame lasted longer than nine days).

Nocturnal and diurnal

Those who prefer the early morning hours have been

called larks, and those who prefer to stay up late have been referred to as owls, but they are all tuned in, more or less, to the twenty-four-hour day.

Nocturnal means "of the night," and nocturnal animals are those whose normal waking hours are at night, and who sleep during the day. Some of them may waken each night with such regularity that it can be timed to the minute; an internal alarm clock tells them precisely when to get up.

Plants can also be nocturnal; the bloom of the vanilla-scented moonflower opens up at night, just once, before withering on the vine.

Human beings are generally diurnal: up during sunlight and asleep through the night.

Noon

On bright days, few people need a clock to tell them when it is high noon. The sun is overhead, and precisely overhead at the Equator. For a few minutes, objects do not throw shadows.

H. D. Thoreau, the American writer who lived

alone in the woods, usually knew by the sun what hour of the day he was "a-fishing in," but occasionally there were other time markers as well: "Was that a farmer's noon horn which sounded from beyond the woods just now?"

For those of us in the digital age of Swatches, the hour of noon remains the one time of day we can still guess by the position of the sun (at least in the months when we are not on daylight saving time, during which the sun is overhead at 1 p.m.).

Astronomers measured the day from noon to noon until 1925. Sailors began their watches at noon. (Those sailors who worked hard keeping watch were likely to earn a "liberty"—an authorized leave from service lasting forty-eight hours or less.)

For most people, though, noon means a midday meal—even if they are not hungry yet, it is still "time for a little something."

Norwegian winter

Norway, a country far to the north, has long, dark

winters. Somehow its name came to be linked with any long-lasting winter, when the snow is very deep. During a Norwegian winter, people say, woodland animals must mix bark with any other food they find simply in order to survive until spring.

On time

To be punctual is a sort of agreement we have in our dealings with others. When we promise to be in a certain place at a certain time, we will be there and so will they—no lies, no weaseling. For most, being prompt is part of a moral code.

Punctuality was once a courtesy and moral obligation, but somewhere along the line, it became a demand. When workers say they "punch the clock," perhaps they are really expressing a half-furious wish, rather than simply talking about a mechanical motion they make at the factory gates each morning and evening.

Despite their starchy, scientific reputation for precision, clocks have been the amusement of many. Lewis Carroll has written about a watch that tells the days, but not the hour; he also points out that a stopped watch is accurate twice a day (if it is fixed on the hour of eight o'clock, twice a day it is exactly right), while a working watch that loses a minute every day will be accurate

only once every two years.

At one time, in certain circles of exclusive gatherings and pretty manners, to be on time was to be too early, and wise were those who arrived fashionably late.

Nowadays, everybody does it.

Once upon a time

Sometimes it looks like a too-familiar way to start a story, a phrase used so much and so often that readers do not even notice it anymore, as if the writer did not have anything better to say.

But, once upon a time, before the days of television or radio or even books, a story was told by firelight, the storyteller hoarsely whispering the words "once upon a time" to people who listened to stories perhaps only once in a blue moon, or who could not read, or who did not know the world beyond their own small domains. The phrase took them away from their present worries and into an enchanted time, when such fairytale celebrities as Sleeping Beauty and Snow White were suspended in time, waiting for spells to be broken and trinkets to work their ways. Such was the power of this phrase that tells of what happened, once, in a time that no longer existed (if it ever did), that we can remember only in words.

In the books by A. A. Milne about a bear named Winnie the Pooh, "once upon a time" translates to "a very long time ago now, about last Friday." Within the pages, time stands still; a reader who met Pooh sixty years ago and a reader who meets him today in the Hundred Acre Wood will find that the days are fairly alike and only the weather changes. When Pooh's friend Christopher Robin learns to read, it is his way of leaving that timeless wood behind and heading off for school, a place very much regulated by mechanical clocks of many shapes and sizes.

Before he goes, Christopher Robin admits that he will be nostalgic for the place. Nostalgia is a sweet mood caused by remembrance of a time gone by, a way of feeling "at home" in a part of the past, and of recalling it fondly, if not always correctly. Clocks and calendars are no barrier for nostalgic tenderness; a piece of music or a scent can send most parents back to their teenage years or even further back to their childhoods. It is a temporary state, however, since being nostalgic requires the person feeling it to be firmly rooted in the present.

Playtime

This is any period of any length in which play takes place. No hour defines its start or its finish; children play when they play, and very young children seem to stop playing only when they are asleep.

To be totally absorbed in play can also mean not to feel time's passing. Parents often forget this, when those who were supposed to be home before dark show up past nightfall.

The hallmark of a game called *Go*, especially popu-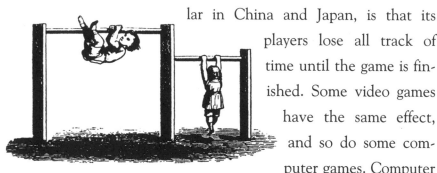lar in China and Japan, is that its players lose all track of time until the game is finished. Some video games have the same effect, and so do some computer games. Computer time, in general, can be extremely captivating and has a speed all its own.

When people grow up, things change. Free time to adults is almost the equivalent of what playtime is to children; most adults "play" on the weekend. Their leisure time is determined by their work schedule, usually Monday through Friday. In other words, adults may get the weekend "off," but only because they have the weekdays "on."

Time off, free time, and vacation time are expressions that now mean time away from regular school or office duties. But "vacation days" comes from a Latin phrase that meant exactly the opposite, *dies*  *vacantes,* or "vacant days." That is what the ancient Romans called the days on which there were no religious holidays and therefore no feasting or rites. On vacant days, they were free to pursue the ordinary undertakings of daily life: work, shopping, whatever.

Puddles of time

Most of us are accustomed to the idea of time as a line we travel on that extends indefinitely behind and before us, or as something that is with us at every moment and surrounds us like a huge ocean. That is not what everyone believes, though. Some people think of time as puddles rather than as an ocean, a lake, or a long line of river water—it is as if some segments of the riverline were erased; or as if time were patches that they can step in and out of like the chalk squares of a game of hopscotch. Stepping "in" and "out" of time can be hard to imagine.

The African people called the Tiv see time as "rooms" they enter, each one for a distinct activity that cannot be interrupted. To make an arrowhead, for instance, a Tiv would go into the activity and not be available for anything else until that deed was done. That is how they "make time" for something. Or, in a more up-to-date example, a person may have it in his or her head to see all episodes of *Twilight Zone* on a certain television channel and will not change programs or leave the room (or the couch) until that mission is accomplished. The Tiv keep their enclosed rooms completely separate and will not embark on another activity without "exiting" or finishing the first one. Outside these rooms, they believe, there is no such thing as time.

Likewise, a runner, frozen at the starting line, does not begin to race until the pistol shot is heard and the stopwatch is on. When the runner crosses the finish line, the stopwatch is frozen—the race has taken place in a pocket of time that seems separate from ordinary clock time.

The starting point and the finish line may be the only things that matter to African people called the

Nuer, who think of the time that comes in the middle (between start and finish) as non-existent, as if it did not happen at all. It is like seeing the entrance of a tunnel and the end of the tunnel, but never the inside of the tunnel. They mark their time by noting the first and the last of their lineage—the most ancient relative and the most recent infant—as if time were an invisible tree. They can see the roots and the leaves, but what is in between does not matter. Or it is like a deck of cards: they can see the top card and the bottom card, but nothing of the cards in between. The top card changes only when family members change, when new faces replace old ones.

Time can be one large pool everyone swims in, several backyard pools strewn over an ocean front, or even separate rooms within houses. It can also be thought of as a series of matrioshka dolls which fit one inside the other, or, according to a British professor named A. N. Whitehead, packed like a nest of boxes of a Chinese toy: the toys, placed one inside the other, all look alike, only the sizes are different. They get smaller and smaller until nothing is left. One box might be sixty times the size of another inside it, in the same way that an hour is sixty times a minute or a minute is sixty times a second, and so on.

Like the chunks-within-chunks of time, stories also can be nested in this fashion. In the storybook known as *1001 Nights*, a brief yarn may be told by one character who himself is part of a tale that yet another storyteller is reciting at a different time and place, in a circle of stories and stories-within-stories that span over centuries.

Reading

It can last ten minutes on the bus on the way to school or an entire rainy morning on the seat by the window—but most readers do not sit down to read for a specific amount of time, except in the classroom.

Book time and clock time generally do not match; it may take two days or more to read a book about something that takes place in one twenty-four-hour day. Readers, totally absorbed in a story, can cover mighty epochs and vast distances, travel back five hundred years, or simply follow through the two worst weeks of a character's life. All this happens in the time it takes to read a book.

Reading time is always "off the clock" as is, in general, television time and movie time. When a sitcom lasts a half-hour or a movie runs one hour and fifty-five minutes, how much time did the characters live through? Were there flashbacks? Were there commercials, during which the action stopped and then started again right where it left off?

Readers and viewers suspend disbelief when they enter the realm of the media. They stop thinking in terms of what is real, logical, and sensible, or in terms of clock time, accounting for every minute that passes, one after the other. In reading, real time and what is called fictional time meet.

Whether reading trash in the bathroom or cliffhangers around bedtime, anyone who has ever put a book down at the moment something terrible is happening to the hero knows that reading time is a distinct chunk of time to move in and out of at will.

Rhythm

One bang of the drum is just noise, two bangs is more noise, but three bangs can be a beat—with a rhythm.

Heartbeats, pulses, a dripping faucet—any beat can

be used as a means for measuring time.

A breath has one cycle per four seconds. In principle, friends can agree to be "on the road in five heartbeats," because a heartbeat has an average of one cycle per second. Perhaps that is why the Tin Man in *The Wizard of Oz* gets a clock instead of the old ticker.

Crickets are known to chirp at a regular pace, and constantly; cells "tick"; and some rhythms in nature are as regular as breathing. One of the most accurate time rhythms is the Binary Pulser, a neutron star that orbits around a collapsing star so fast and so regularly, that it forms a "pulse" or beat about seventeen times per second, that scientists use it as a very precise nature clock.

But about that faucet (*drip drip drip*). . . . Perhaps the quintessential water clock, the dripping faucet seems to create in every listener (*drip drip drip*) anxiety about past bungles and all the time that is going down the drain; a state of panic (*drip drip drip*) over future events; or the awful looming sense of wide-awake waiting. Few people find it (*drip drip drip*) soothing. It has been linked with torture, and it is the ultimate erosive weapon. This is not scientifically sound, but one can almost say that water plus solid rock equals the sands of time slipping away.

One of the more famous natural rhythms is the circadian rhythm. The word "circadian" comes from the Latin *circa*, meaning "approximately," and *dias*, meaning "day." A day is considered one of nature's beats. The rhythm of "almost a day" can be best understood by those who have lived in sealed caves, places where there is no night or day, no weather, no clocks, and no time cues. Such cave dwellers have almost always gone through a cycle of more than the twenty-four-hour rhythm everyone else is used to. But one Frenchman lived in a cave in Del Rio, Texas, for six months without a clock, and his circadian rhythms were like no other's. His days lasted from twenty hours to forty-eight hours. No one told him he was staying up too late, and so he was not.

Sacred time

To believers in religion, five sacred minutes of praying is worth as much as or more than the rest of the day. Prayer time may be the ancestor of what we now call quality time. Five minutes of enjoying a good book or being with a loved one can be worth a whole day of chores or tedious work.

Time can be spent privately (with oneself or with God) or publicly (with others). Officially, monks, nuns, and others prayed publicly during the canonical hours; the prayers of the rest of the day were considered private, no matter how many people chanted them.

Religious or not, people of all cultures have sacred moments, private and public. Some are formalized into rituals and holidays, and some remain in the minds and souls of people who share common values, likes and dislikes; and still others are shared by most, if not all, human beings.

Season

Whether it is the first sighting of candy corn in store windows or the first sighting of southbound birds, the clues that autumn is in the air abound without anyone mentioning the word "September." The school year passes in a calendar of scratched-off days, but seasons seem to pass by painlessly. Each one has its symbols and signs, from brightly colored leaves and gathered stalks of corn to maypoles and tight new buds.

Prehistoric people, from about 35,000 B.C. onward, recorded their observations of the seasons in paintings with subjects such as salmon at spawning time and stags in their autumn rut.

The ancient Egyptians had three seasons. The first did not begin until the Nile had flooded the lands on which they intended to plant crops. This first season was known as inundation, the second as seed time, and the last as the harvest.

For the Saulteaux people, a group of Chippewa living in southern Canada, the spring season means moving to maple groves for sugaring time. The summer season means that sometime in August they will relocate again to the wild-rice beds where they will participate in the harvest.

The appearance of a worm launches the seasonal cycle of planting for the Trobriander Islanders of New Guinea. The palolo worm, which lives underwater in coral reefs, makes a yearly visit to the surface of the wa-

ter for three or four nights. Its visit is followed by a festival; participants honor the worm's appearance by roasting and devouring it. Trobrianders then name the month in which the worm appeared *Milamala*; that is to say, they name the month only after it has taken place.

Sometimes the meaning of seasons is turned inside out. In the fashion industry, designers must prepare clothing months in advance of a season to give stores time to buy, ship, and stock the outfits. Their seasons fall exactly opposite what many people expect of the calendar: designers have their spring styles ready for fall fashion shows and their fall styles ready in spring. With the clocks on their backs, they have to stay one step ahead.

In these days of goodly gains, to be "in season" means to be "out of season."

Shank of the afternoon

The shank of the afternoon (or the evening) is its waxing or waning moments—the last few minutes before the sun sets, for example, when people's thoughts turn to the onset of night. The shank is the beginning or the end of any period of time.

Sick day

This is a day out of school or work, due to a convincing case of symptoms or a convincing case for gaining unscheduled time off. Once in a while the symptoms that put a student at death's door in the early morning miraculously recede shortly thereafter or sometime in the late afternoon.

But for real illness, and the common cold in particular, there is no schedule for recovery; healing, with few exceptions, takes its own time and no one as yet can speed it up. Did the medicine help, or did the use of medicine just coincide with the period of getting well?

Sleep

There are as many timespans for sleeping as there are people who need to rest. Who decides what is bedtime, and what is only a nap or a Sunday morning lie-in?

There is nothing like a little snooze after lunch, and thus the time-honored tradition of the siesta was born. Businesses all over Italy and the rest of the Mediterranean close up for lunch and do not reopen until late afternoon.

What was once simply a custom now has a basis in science; the body's biological rhythms ebb around this time of day, no matter how much sleep a person has had or what was on the lunch menu.

The need for a nap, students know, is one of the afternoon's hardest won battles, with a dull geography lesson and Morpheus (the Greek god of sleep) on one side and only a fear of punishment on the other. It makes the natural world, where animals hibernate according to set biological cycles, with no one to bother them, look

downright civilized.

Rip Van Winkle intended to sleep about forty winks, which would have been a very short rest indeed (wink forty times and see how long it takes). His most famous nap lasted, instead, nearly twenty years.

Snail's pace

Anyone who has ever watched this gastropod creep sluggishly and clammily along would never want to be called a snail. Its rate of progress down the primrose path varies from one species to another, and has never been scientifically clocked, but it is universally agreed that snails are slower than molasses. We can only wonder, though, if the snail finds that people travel too fast.

Snow day

A joyous occasion that is nowhere to be found on any calendar. In the United States, this longed-for day off from school, and sometimes work, happens as many (or as few) times in winter as snow disrupts buses, schedules, and traffic.

Weather forecasters may try to put snow on the clock—they predict, scan satellite photos, test conditions, and then grandly state which day the blizzard will arrive. But snow mostly comes when it comes, not when the weatherlady says so.

Schoolchildren in New York City may get more snow days than those in St. Paul, Minnesota, simply because New York is not as equipped for heavy snowfall as is St. Paul.

Snow underfoot, some say, makes time spent walking seem much longer than it would on dry pavement. But everyone knows that a snow day, at home reading or sledding, will seem to go faster than a school day, no matter how interesting the classwork or flexible the schedules.

Solar heartbeat

The sun's heartbeat, it comes approximately once every eleven years. When it comes, scientists compare the highs and lows of sunspot activity.

Soldag

On *Soldag*, or Sun Day, the sun returns to the sky after months of winter darkness in Scandinavia. It can almost be said of the residents in this part of the world that they have just one real "Sunday" a year. Such a day is cause for celebration, or even a day off, except for the cows—it is a well known fact that cows do not rest on Sundays.

Solstice

An astronomer and an anthropologist might break in at this point to stop and explain at great length that this term has to do with the sun's position in the sky in relation to Earth. Forget it. What is most important about the solstice is its associations with the longest and shortest days of the year north of the Equator.

By the modern calendar, the summer solstice is around June 22, when the sun is highest in the sky (at its zenith) and gives people in the Northern Hemisphere more hours of daylight than they know what to do with. Ancient books say that the color associated with the summer solstice is resin (yellowish brown), because the heat of the sun makes the oak sweat this substance.

The winter solstice occurs when the sun is at its lowest place in the sky, or at its nadir; it makes those same people feel as if they are in near perpetual duskiness. It happens around December 22.

The sun rises in late morning and starts to set almost before school is out. Old texts say that the color of this season is piebald (blotchy black-and-white), because of the white snow piled up against the door and the chimneys black with soot.

Other expressions for the summer solstice and the winter solstice are midsummer and midwinter, mentioned above.

Sunwise

Of course, the sun does not rise or set; it is Earth that rotates. Sunwise is the direction the sun seems to take through the sky.

The sun—whose influence on human beings from time immemorial would take volumes to discuss—has been associated with many life-giving and life-altering events and ideas. And it has been associated with god, kings, and even the lowly dung beetles that rise with the first rays of the sun.

A typical custom showing the sun's role in daily life and the world at large occurs at sunset and again at sunrise in a Mexican village. Children who are descendants of the Maya stand at the entrance to the hut of their elders, feet together, with arms folded across their breasts and tips of their fingers under their forearms. In this

way, they perform the ceremonial greeting twice a day. The tradition is so old that it can be found on ancient painted vessels and in sculpture.

When the sun appears to drop below the horizon, night is on its way. Present-day Maya begin their burials at sunset in order to make sure the coffin is lowered into the ground in the moments right after the sun has entirely left the sky. Any sooner, they believe, and the soul of the dead person will remain on Earth.

The carved baboons that decorate Egyptian temples were placed to catch the very first rays of light each morning. Why have these animals been so honored? The sound of baboons chattering and crying with first light, like a rooster's crow in the morning, has made them a symbol of sunrise.

In ancient Egyptian mythology the scarab beetle represents the rising sun, some say because of the sphere it constructs in which to deposit its eggs. It buries the

The Egyptian sun god travels the night sky in a boat.

sphere in the ground, just as the sun disappears below the horizon each night; when the eggs hatch out of the earth, new beetles emerge into daylight from the darkness of the ground and the sun rises seemingly from this event. And there are more down-to-earth associations with the sun's journey. Some believed that the goddess of the sky swallows the sun for the night; it then travels through her body until morning, when it comes out through her lower end—and she thus gives birth to the sun god yet again.

Teatime

Even though the British have precise hours in which to

consume the national beverage—and pride themselves on such precision—most people have a "cuppa" *whenever* the urge hits. In *Alice's Adventures in Wonderland,* by Lewis Carroll, the Mad Hatter tells Alice when the clock gets stuck, "It's always tea-time."

When there is honey in the house, it is "time-for-a-little-something" in any part of Winnie the Pooh's day, unless it is "very nearly teatime, and then they had a Very Nearly tea, which is one you forget about afterwards. . . ."

In a completely different mood, English teatime can be a very formal and lofty affair. So is the Japanese's teatime—it can even be more stately, and, some say, has a little more grace. Teatime in Japan, or *chan-no-yu,* is a gathering marked by great formality and care.

Since the twelfth century, after Japanese Zen monks adopted the Chinese custom of tea drinking to keep themselves awake during meditation, the Japanese have made tea-tippling an art form. Those invited to the tea garden are led down paths and offered scenic views to keep them in the "right mood," such as in the mood of "a landscape in clouded moonlight, with a half-gloom between the trees."

Tempo

The equivalent of nature's rhythm, a tempo is the speed at which a musical composition is played.

Big names and small have linked time and music in the largest and smallest of schemes. An ancient Greek mathematician thought of time as caused by the rhythm of the planets as they revolve; he called it the "music of the spheres." And the fruit fly's protein has a beat that is so perfectly in tempo that it has been likened to sand in an hourglass and scientists use it as a unit of measure; they call it the "song" of the fruit fly.

There is a time beat to every kind of music. But one does not always have to "beat time" to learn music. For the Japanese, there is no such beating of time; perhaps it is more of an embrace. In general, Japanese music has what is known as an open score. It has no time rules and restrictions, and the beat, if there is one, is left to the individual musician to "jazz" around with—serenely, and from the depth of the heart.

Time of the angels

To an angel, even time-lapse photography of a plant moving from seed to full bloom would be too slow; seed and bloom would exist at once, in a flash.

toto simul

Toto simul: *all at once*

Angel time, or "time of the angels," as people in medieval times called it, is when things happen all at once—beginning, middle, and end. In this time, there would be little or no difference between milliseconds and millennia.

If, for most people in those days, time flow was like traveling one street at a time or one road at a time, angel time was like being on every street and road at the same time, not only in this town or the next, but in all towns and villages the world over. And, when a year passes, people age; angels will not.

The composer Mozart, it is said, experienced his music in this way. He did not hear it in his head note by note, one after the other, but in its entirety, beginning and end and every note in between in the same instant. Perhaps it was like looking on a valley that stretched below and seeing the whole thing all at once, instead of coming across one tree at a time or one rock at a time.

Angels journey through, or dwell in, the "everlasting," a word generally described as "the window between worldly time and eternity."

Timekeepers

Here are three timekeepers, among whom there are

worlds of difference: a scientific timekeeper, a poetic timekeeper, and a mythical timekeeper.

The first is none other than Big Ben, the large bell in the clock tower and grand messenger of the standard time charted in Greenwich, England. That heap of metal's echo is heard throughout the world. That is clock time.

The second is but a gentle soul—the lamplighter. At sunset, it is the lamplighter on his rounds who is the time-keeper in Robert Louis Stevenson's tribute to the task:

My tea is nearly ready and the sun has left the sky;
It's time to take the window to see Leerie going by;
For every night at teatime and before you take your
    seat,
With lantern and with ladder he comes posting up
    the street.

Time Devours All

The third is the Greek god Chronos—also known as the Roman god Saturn—from whom comes the word "chronology." He was the son of Uranus and is most famous for devouring his own children. (We know about wasting time and using up time, and we have heard about beating time and killing time, but eating time? Or time eating itself up? Or its children? There had to be a better way.)

Twilight

In the days before electricity, those on a darkening path at evening's twilight were likely to quicken their steps. Shopkeepers lit their lanterns and prepared to close for the night.

No one can say exactly when it is twilight, the time when the sunlight is dim and diffused by dust and Earth's atmosphere. It comes twice a day: as the first gray light between nighttime and sunrise—dawn—and between sunset and nighttime—dusk.

People once believed that during this time there was

an opening between this world and the next, which may be why twilight is also a way of describing the later years of a person's life or career.

In more superstitious times, the twilight period, or gloaming, was a murky one, in which both ne'er-do-wells and various spirits were on their way to or back from mischief. It was not a time for decent folk to be outside of the home or away from the hearth.

A successful television series focused on the effects of entering the Twilight Zone; almost no one fared well there.

Watchman

"Watch" did not always mean the funny little disc people wear strapped to their wrists or dangling inside a vest pocket, nor was a watchman a small, portable television set.

A watch originally had to do not with clocks, but with the idea of "keeping watch" at night or "watching out." It came to mean the way a night was divided into sections for those taking turns standing guard.

In China, the night consisted of five watches of varying lengths. The Romans also divided the night into watches, in a system that is still used in armed forces around the world. In fourteenth-century Europe, citizens banded together, policing their streets to discourage any thieves or wastrels who had penetrated the city's gates for a night of wrongdoing.

The idea of someone remaining awake and alert for the benefit of others through the dark hours is as old as it is noble; it is commemorated by a Dutch artist named Rembrandt in a famous painting called "The Night Watch."

Week

Not always the same old seven days, a week has meant different day counts at different times. These days it is the label given to a cycle of work and leisure or a cycle of school and playtime.

In the United States, the school week is five days on and two days off (ignoring weeks with holidays); the work week is more often than not tied to a similar schedule. But not everyone agrees which day is the Sabbath. It is a matter of religious belief; for some it is Sunday; for others, Saturday; and for some others, Friday. Still, there are relatively few people in the world who do not now accept the seven-day clump.

The seven-day week comes our way from holy books, but the days themselves bear almost uniformly what are called pagan names derived from old Scandi-

navian languages: Sunday, after the sun; Monday, after the moon; Tuesday, for the god Tiw (also known as Mars); Wednesday, for the god Woden; Thursday for the god Thor; Friday, for the goddess Freya; and Saturday, for the god Saturn.

Rather than using these pre-Christian names, the religious order called the Quakers chose to give each day a number instead, beginning with Sunday as the First Day, Monday as the Second Day, and so on to the Seventh Day.

But the seven-day week has not always been in use. It is not an actual law or rule; it is another convention, or an accepted way of doing things. In 1929, a four-day work week was implemented in Soviet Russia, with a fifth day for rest. It lasted only two years. And perhaps the shortest week of all—three days—was adopted by the ancient Colombians of South America. (Just imagine if two of those days were the weekend. That is a long time to do homework.)

To commemorate a new history with a new calendar after the French Revolution some two hundred years ago, people temporarily went from a seven-day week to a ten-day week, and each day was ten hours, each hour one hundred minutes, and each minute one hundred seconds. The Sabbath took place on the tenth day. This followed the schedule of the ancient Greeks, who also kept a ten-day week.

Year

The word "year" means different things to different people; it always has.

Strictly speaking, one year equals the 365 days between New Year's Day and New Year's Eve, or the twelve months between one birthday and the next.

But only ten months are needed to make up the school year, from September through June in the United States, a fact which pleases some students.

No matter when a year is launched—New Year's Day, a birthday, or the first day of school—it always brings with it the chance for fresh starts and new beginnings. That may be why the same word is used for "year" and "world" by the Yokuts and the Yuki, two groups of

North American native people. When a new year starts, they believe they have a whole new world to work with. This may mean that they experience the end of the world once a year, but then, so do most people, in a way. Every New Year's Eve, people ring out the old year and ring in the new. The ceremony is more than a simple chiming of midnight—it is a mood, a moment of anticipation—perhaps optimism—and rebirth.

A fresh start can be as easy as shopping for school clothes, but it can also be more complicated. In years past, people so longed for a chance to start over that they took what we might think of as drastic measures. The same new government in France that changed the week to ten days on the heels of the French Revolution changed September 22, 1792 to Year 1, Day 1. It may have been a way of saying that their country, which had just emerged from a bloody civil war, was reborn, with a brand new history.

It was a noble gesture, but that system of year-keeping lasted less than 20 years. There are probably many reasons why it did not work, but one of them may have been that staying in step with the rest of the world means using the same calendar. Imagine a Londoner and a Parisian agreeing to meet on a certain day; if each had a different calendar, how could they make a date? On January 1, 1808, France reverted to the system still in use today in France and in most nations of the world.

In classical Greece, the years were not numbered, but instead named for ruling magistrates, and instead of counting a year at a time, they counted in an Olympiad, or one four-year period. And in the eleventh century B.C., the word "year" also meant harvest. The Roman year began in March and ended in December; until the Gregorian calendar replaced the Julian calendar in 1752, the English began their year in spring on what was then called the 25th of March, or the Day of Annunciation.

The sacred lodges constructed by both the Algonquin and the Sioux peoples represent their ideas about the year as well as about the universe at large. A year is a journey in four directions: east, west, north, and south. The lodge is therefore built with a window and door on each of four sides, ensuring that such a journey is possible.

For the Native Americans of southern Arizona, the new year began with the first appearance of cottonwood leaves, which occurs sometime in February. A year in the lives of the Aztecs and Maya lasted 260 days, or one *lamat,* while the new year for the Northwest Indians is heralded by the return of salmon to their territory.

Most people mark the year's passing with a birthday, and they talk about their age in terms of years. But long ago, the English playwright Shakespeare thought of people's lives as composed of phases, not years, known as the seven ages of man: infant, schoolboy, lover, soldier, justice, an older man with a "shrunk shank," and finally, a hollow, ancient presence in a state of second "childishness." Another old-fashioned way of thinking

The seven ages of man

about aging, without using the year as a measurement, divides life into childhood, youth, prime (as in "the prime of one's life"), and old age.

Yesterday, today, and tomorrow

It is not every day that people sit around talking about the past or the future—both times sound so far away; but the past is as recent as a split second ago, and the future is only a pinch ahead of right now. It is far easier to use the bread-and-butter words for the past and future—yesterday and tomorrow.

For some people, there are no words for yesterday and tomorrow, past and future, or before and after. Perhaps "now" is the only time they know.

For most people, now is gone even before the word is off their lips. There is *almost* no such thing as now. It is simply too fleeting.

For the ancient Greeks, time was essentially "now" or "not now." The time of "not now" could be either the past or the future, since they had no notion of history as something that had started in the past, included the present, and would extend into the future. For them time—and history—followed the path of a circle rather than a straight line, cyclic rather than linear. Whether an event had happened one thousand years earlier, or the day before yesterday, it was still part of "not now."

In some stories, King Arthur's court wizard, Merlin, was said to be going backward in time. He knew the future because he had lived through it, and when he died, it was back to the future for him.

To the Navajo people of the southwestern United States, events that happen in the past and future are all in the same place, not in two different places. And in the African language of Luganda, events are placed in time by saying they happened either in the current twenty-four-hour period or before that; if something occurred twenty-three hours ago, it is still part of the present, but if it occurred twenty-five hours ago, it was in the past.

One group of Amazonians believe that the future is at their backs, where they cannot see it. They think of the past as standing in front of them, where they may view it calmly, for they know what it holds.

The future is a long stretch ahead, too foggy to see or to know. Just as the headlights of a car light up only a portion of the road ahead at night, people experience only a limited domain of time.

Still, for most people, past, present, and future are inseparable; it is impossible to discuss one without the other two.

"Duration" is time people feel or experience, rather

than measure by the clock. The equivalent French word, *Durée*, is a bit more animated—it means that past, present, and future are experienced together as a whole, as something the French call "lived time." If this sounds like a magician's sleight of hand, it is not. If a boy is eating dinner, he will not say "I had my soup in the past, I'm having my main course in the present, and will have my dessert in the future"; all of it is dinner, just dinner—*one* experience, in one chunk of time.

A reader on page 22 of a novel will most certainly be aware of what has already happened in the plot (past), and intends to turn the page to learn more (future), otherwise, the point of reading is lost.

Yesterdaytodayandtomorrow is like a trip on a three-car train traveling along the railroad track. In the middle car is a person in the present. She cannot go into the car in front, which is the future; she cannot take a walk into the caboose, which is the past. Yet all three cars are linked and headed in the same direction. As the eighteenth-century English poet William Blake wrote, "I see the Past, Present, & Future existing all at once/Before me."

Father Time with scythe and auroboros, the wheel of time

Time Out:
Curios, Trivia, and
Second Thoughts

The word "clock" comes from an Italian word of Celtic origin, *clocea*, meaning bell tower. Clocks have traditionally replaced or been perched next to the bells (church bells, mostly) that had so agreeably peeled out the periods of the day. But clocks did not entirely take over the rhythms of the day.

In the book called *Gulliver's Travels,* the little people known as Lilliputians believe that Gulliver's watch is his god, so often does he consult it. To them, the relatively tiny timekeeping device looks like something mightier than this giant of a man who cannot make a move without it. They may have been right about one thing. It is hard to make a move without knowing what time it is, right down to the last digital second. But perhaps they were wrong about the other thing. There is nothing tiny about time. It is huge. It should usually be spelled with a capital "T." But when scientists try to talk about it, they use an eensy, weensy, mousy "t" in the notations they make in their calculations, if only to make it small and manageable enough to control and tally. It is not a word, this "t," but it stands for a number: $t = 2$ seconds, or $t = 7$ hours, or 22 days, or 100 billion trillion years. So many zeroes and fractions pile up that it becomes pointless to keep counting.

In some parts of the world, bells have tolled the hour since the eighth or ninth century, but in the United States, in more recent times, sirens replaced noon bells. Several decades ago, at the height of what has been called the Cold War, sirens went off at high noon all over the country, to test air-raid equipment. They were part of many cities' civil defense warning systems, to be used in case another country chose to bomb the United States by air. Now, even the sirens have fallen into disuse.

There has been much disagreement on the subject of how long days are and when they start. Both the Greeks and the Babylonians believed that the day began with the rise of the sun (though some sources have the Babylonians' day starting at sunset, as do days on the Jewish calendar). People have said that the Egyptians counted days from midnight to midnight (not midnight as 12:00 a.m., but the time of night that everyone agreed could be thought of as midnight), while others point to sunrise as the beginning of the day, when the sun god Osiris began his daily boat journey through the sky, his cargo the disc of the sun.

Another way of referring to sunrise and sunset is to call them the hours of the Angelus, which are similar to the canonical hours. An Angelus bell rings at morning, noon, and evening, calling out the times for specific prayers.

The sun has held importance for many. *Tekohanane* means "daylight" to the Zuni of the southwestern United States, but it also means life. Both the Zuni and Hopi had sun watchers, priests who kept track of time and exalted the sun each time it rose. Even in modern times, regulated by the clock, most people do not think of the new day as beginning at 12:01 a.m., but at sunrise.

Most people know about sundials, but *gnomons*, or so-called "sun sticks" are still used in Tibet. The Roman version of a gnomon was a *hemispherium* (which was replaced in the sixteenth century by a chalice or goblet). This half-globe was hollow and inscribed on the inside with measurements to be read according to the sun's position. Water clocks were invented as a way of making certain everyone got a fair shake from the Athenian courts of law; the gnomon's and hemispherium's solar day was naturally longer in the summer, and those pleading their cases therefore had more time to argue. A *merkhet* was the Egyptian equivalent of the gnomon, but was used at night, with the stars instead of the sun.

Dawn is the part of the day ruled by the Greek goddess Eos, but it was an Egyptian goddess of that hour who was said to moan and groan outside a dead pharaoh's temple many centuries ago.

It is not always the number of dawns people note to keep track of time. A Cree Indian would not want to work the night shift or do any moonlighting since his tradition would not account for the nights on which he could not see the moon (if there was no moon, the night did not count).

Over two hundred years ago, Teutonic tribes in northern Europe kept track of the passing days by counting nights, using units that led to the eighteenth-century expressions "fortnight" (fourteen nights) and "sennight" (seven nights).

In the sixth century B.C., a famous Greek teacher named Heraclitus was the first to associate the name of the child god Aion with time and change: "Time is a child playing a board game; to a child belongs dominion." The bones of sheep were used in knucklebones, a game similar to jacks that Heraclitus liked to play with children. Perhaps it was his days with youthful companions that inspired him to compare entire civilizations to a few rounds of dreads and noughts (or crosses and zeroes, like tic-tac-toe) which, between two good players, can be played to infinity without a clear winner.

No matter how industrious they may be, bees do not have a sense of the past or the future. According to one scientist, the bee's sense of now, or the present moment, may span from five to ten minutes, just long enough for it to tell the other bees the location of the most recently discovered flower delicacy.

In some parts of the world, much can happen in the blink of an eye. For example, for the Jains people of India, a *rajju* is the distance a god can journey in six months if he is traveling at the speed of approximately two million *yojanas* a blink or ten million *yojanas* a second.

In one method of Chinese daykeeping, the slot of time now known as 3 a.m. to 11 a.m. was thought of as spring, 11 a.m. to 5 p.m. as summer, 5 p.m. to 11 p.m. as autumn, and 11 p.m. to 3 a.m. as winter.

According to the psychologist Sigmund Freud, there is

no place for the natural time flow and the clock in dreams—there is no real time.

In Indian mythology, the *Mahayuga* is a cycle of twelve thousand divine years; as each divine year lasts 360 of what most people call a year, one cosmic cycle has a total of 4,320,000 years. The Greeks considered thirty-six thousand years to be one Great Year (*Annus Magnus*), a grand cycle at the end of which the world reverted to some sort of cosmic "square one"; it went back to the beginning.

It is said that the Greek works of Thespis, the "first actor" of dramatic plays, were staged only in open daylight, in the morning in particular, because of the quality of sunlight in the public square. Meanwhile, the secret celebrations of the Eleusinian mysteries (religious rites of the ancient Greeks) were nocturnal—always held under cover of darkness. During Shakespeare's time, plays were performed late in the afternoon, if only for the angle of the light on the stage.

In a book about games and playtime, a man named Johan Huizinga suggested that to know how to play is one of the foundations of culture. He also related playtime to children's natural rhythms and said that the end to game time is decided according to what game is played and by the children themselves, and not by a fixed schedule. A famous Greek philosopher said that the only reason to work was so that there would be time for fun; and that people are not only required to work well but also to play well.

"Gloaming" is another name for a sedate hour of twilight. An American poet named Robert Frost poignantly puts this word to use, perhaps making reference to time accumulation or aging and running out of time: "Do you know me in the gloaming, / Gaunt and dusty gray with roaming?" Time has often been thought of as gray-haired.

In most parts of the world, the new year begins January 1, a system that comes from the Egyptians, who started the solar year with the rising in the night sky of Sirius (the morning and evening star, which guides travelers). For the Chinese, February is the month of the new year .

❧

In India, a fire altar may be constructed according to specific ideas about the year. An enclosure is built from 360 bricks, one for each night of the year, and another 360 *yajasmati* bricks for each of 360 days.

❧

A year in the lives of the Aztecs and Maya lasted 260 days, or one *lamat*. The words "day" and "year" are often used interchangeably when related to some mythologies—perhaps that is why some sources say that one lamat lasts 260 years. Some descendants of the Maya, such as the Qiché Indians of Guatemala, keep both the 260-day year and a 360-day year, which allows them to keep pace with sacred rites as well as civil ones.

❧

It has been said that peasants and children work less by stiff, man-made restrictions and more according to nature's restrictions: light and dark, change of climate, and appetite or lack of it. Accustomed to toiling to the rhythms of the seasons (long days in summer, shorter days in winter), peasants feared or hated the clock. Their workdays grew longer, usually without compensation. One of the many names time and the clock are called, to this day, is "taskmaster." "On the clock," the day's events go past mechanically, as if people were part of an assembly line or a gigantic ticker tape. C. S. Lewis, the religious author of *The Chronicles of Narnia*, called Hell "a murky, sooty town, always close to the end of the workday."

❧

When mechanized clocks came into the scene, only the wealthy or members of royalty owned them, as did the Church.

❧

On a building wall in New York City there is a digital clock that tells the hours, the minutes, the seconds, the milliseconds, and even microseconds and beyond in a line of numbers turning from left to right. It is like one big scorecard, with the numbers increasing, racing past, going higher and higher, piling on with otherworldly speed and ferocity, and then, silently, hastily, turning over to zeroes at midnight. But the relief is fleeting because the breathtaking count begins all over again. On the left, the number of the hour sits still, unchanging and unmoving, while on the right the numbers race by so fast that the eye cannot discern any one digit. Time is both stopped and crashing past, all in the blinking of lights. It is easy to be hypnotized by the sight, until the eye moves just a little farther to the right. There, is an office building full of workers; below, are shoppers on the street, and parents pushing baby carriages; cabs honk and messengers bike and street crews block traffic; a group of schoolchildren hold hands on the way to a museum; construction workers place the underpinnings for another skyscraper deep into the earth. They do not give that clock even a passing glance.

Bibliography

AVENI, ANTHONY F. *Empires of Time*. New York: Basic Books, 1989.

BAUDEZ, CLAUDE and SIDNEY PICASSO. *Lost Cities of the Maya*. New York: Harry N. Abrams, 1992.

BOUSLOUGH, JOHN. *National Geographic*. "The Enigma of Time." March 1990.

CARROLL, LEWIS. *Alice's Adventures in Wonderland & Through the Looking Glass*. Various editions.

COVENEY, PETER and ROGER HIGHFIELD. *The Arrow of Time*. New York: Ballantine Books, 1991.

DE GRAZIA, SEBASTIAN. *Of Time, Work and Leisure*. Garden City: Doubleday, 1964.

EARLE, ALICE MORSE. *Sundials and Roses of Yesterday*. New York: The Macmillan Co,. 1902.

FRASER, J. T. *Time, the Familiar Stranger*. Redmond, WA: Tempus Books, 1987.

⸻, ed. *The Voices of Time*. Amherst: University of Massachusetts Press, 1981.

FRAZER, SIR JAMES GEORGE. *The Golden Bough*. New York: Macmillan, 1922.

GIFFORD, DON. *The Farther Shore: A Natural History of Perception, 1798-1984*. New York: Atlantic Monthly Press, 1990.

GOODWIN, JOE, et al., eds. *Fire of Life: The Smithsonian Book of the Sun*. New York: Smithsonian Exposition Books, 1981.

HALL, EDWARD T. *The Dance of Life*. New York: Doubleday, 1983.

HUIZINGA, JOHAN. *Homo Ludens: A Study of the Play Element in Culture*. Boston: Beacon Press, 1955

MILNE, A. A. *Winnie the Pooh*. New York: Dutton, 1926.

MODY, N. H. N. *Japanese Clocks*. Rutland, VT: Charles E. Tuttle, 1967.

RYBCZYNSKI, WITOLD. *Waiting for the Weekend*. New York: Viking, 1991.

THOREAU, HENRY DAVID. *Walden, and On the Duty of Civil Disobedience*. New York: Holt, Rhinehart and Winston, 1948.

VERCOUTTER, JEAN. *The Search for Ancient Egypt*. New York: Harry N. Abrams, 1992.

WATERHOUSE, J. M., D. S. MINORS, and M. E. WATERHOUSE. *Your Body Clock*. New York: Oxford University Press, 1990.

WRIGHT, LAWRENCE. *Clockwork Man*. New York: Horizon Press, 1969.

SOURCES:

8, Musée Conde. Giraudon, Paris; 15, Bartholomaeus Angelicus, *De Proprietatibus Rerum*. Lyon, 1485; 37, Ursual Schleicher-Benz, *Lindauer Bilderbogen* 8. Jan Thorbecke Verlag, Simaringen; 38, A. M. Hind, *Early Italian Engraving*; 44, Coverdale's Bible, 1535; 50, 51, 99, George Cruikshank; 53, Athanasius Kircher, *Magnes sive de Arte Magnetica Opus Tripartum*; frontispiece, 63, *The Kalander of Shepherdes*, 1506; 111, Woodcut from Petrarch, Gregorio de Gregorii, Trieste, 1508.